NIGHTS IN SON]

by Liezl Villanueva

Nights in Sonder City

Liezl Villanueva

Published by Draft2Digital, 2024.

NIGHTS IN SONDER CITY

First edition. May 1, 2024.

Copyright © 2024 Liezl Villanueva.

ISBN: 979-8224996483

Written by Liezl Villanueva.

Chapter I
The Self

Prisms

Here she comes—

a tread in the sky, absent of meringue clouds,

she glides softly, her swings unproud,

a silent bee in the dark, a sprite without a doubt,

her gleeful scent like an unkempt pout.

Here she paints—

dyes ink her stems, from finger to finger,

her canvas a woven quilt of ether,

light floods her heart for soulful reasons,

do painters make prisms?

Underwater Hymns

Grappling a sense of wonder,

beats fell out of my mouth.

Like drizzle to downpour,

rhyme spilled in galore.

I kicked my way to the surface,

sang songs every moon phase.

Awestruck with your world,

I dwelled atop jutting rocks.

Tunes sat at the tip of my tongue,

ready to dance in a hymn unsung.

The Butterfly Nebula

You are one story yet to be told,

Mighty highs and lows,

Here we stumble and go.

Rise up, up, up, with the stars,

There you will see

How far you've come.

When asterisks no longer matter,

You put them on pedestals.

Crying on crystals

You remain strong, indomitable,

Each milestone carves one heart

Too stiff, too kind

What else can you do to make it better?

Write a letter?

Or jump to another dimension?

Oh, sweet lady,

Where you go is where you will meet your destiny.

Pedal Pushers

Tick, tick, click

The wheels are ready

You follow the trail

Up, up, up

Down, down, down

The mountains and seas.

You crane your neck

For the road ahead

Loud horns and cricket noises

Accompany you to the edge

Of every summit or pitfall.

Each push of your feet

Each turn of your handlebar

Makes your heart happier than ever

For what is life without adventure?

When you reach the zenith,

Don't be afraid to look down,

See the earth from the rise,

With your bicycle,

You can do anything,

Go anywhere you want.

Pedal pushers will help you

Look what's yonder,

Point a place in the map,

So I can look for you down under.

Heroes of Papyrus

I once adored a boy

Made of words and metaphors.

He's not a cookie-cutter–

For the ships he sailed,

For the wars he fought,

For the planes he flew in Adriatic Sea.

If you look too closely,

You will realize that

He's the brother you haven't seen in ages.

He's the neighbor who helped you

When no one else didn't offer a thing.

He's a stranger you thought was bad

When, in fact, he meant to do good.

Heroes of papyrus aren't paper-thin

Nor are they figments of a desperate,

Moony-eyed artist.

They feed a hungry heart,

From poets to novelists.

Generations after generations,

Piles of ink blotted

And spilled for building these heroes.

Alas! I made a mistake.

Does life imitate art?

Or does art imitate life?

Beautifully Cursed Appendage

A dragonfly once perched on a windowsill.

Its wings fluttered, lurched,

Grew silent as it searched for its meal.

Once it flew from a farm field,

Bringing with it a strip of light

To the Farmer's Guild.

Who else would want a dark dragonfly?

Unbeknownst to its companions,

It carried a broken wing

For far longer than a millennium.

Yet it thrived, flew past lakes,

From cornfields to rose gardens.

Purified with the sight,

Its round eyes afforded

What any other dragonfly couldn't see.

Panoramas of blurry nature

Made it dance in glee,

If only, if only

Everyone had the power to see,

It would never trade

Its black, broken wing,

Even for a beautiful tree.

Bird's-eye View

The sky lights up with a thousand eyes

Staring at you from above.

Stars, planets, asteroids,

All wait for you to–

Look up,

Smile, laugh,

Or even cry.

You whispered to me once

The mysteries of the universe.

What happens inside a black hole?

What makes up dark matter?

How the universe started

Makes the scientists go mad.

You laughed and said,

They are fools

For playing gods.

It is enough if you die

Without seeing the multiverse.

You will be happy in your death

When another star is named.

These breakthroughs don't matter to you;

To get a glimpse of them

Through the naked eye

Is the greatest gift of all.

Morrow

Champagnes of yesterday,

Cheap red wines of today,

I'll wait till the morrow.

Our sorrows come full circle,

Anxiety leaps in a throttle,

I'll pause till our embrace.

Tomorrow, we'll see

What it means to be free;

I'll stay till we meet.

Profound at Nineteen

Like an hourglass,

our story began in minutiae.

Like blacksmiths forging metals,

we must keep these feelings at bay.

What ifs turned to how are yous,

enemies to lovers to beaus.

Confidence strengthened us,

you and me together in a sea of fuss.

Slowly but surely, a bond forged within,

profound at nineteen.

Amplified

My mind keeps ticking

It's louder than any bell.

Wired differently from birth, we can see

How unique are we.

Our thoughts are dominoes

They move sinuously

From one point to another, perhaps—

From one person to the other?

What does it feel like?

To cry,

To say goodbye,

To move in synch,

With people we feel closest to,

With moments we lost hope to.

Our thoughts are codes—

They scream to fight turpitude

They sing songs to lure us from our humble abodes.

Patintero

It was the fifth week of summer,

July of two thousand three,

In a muddy rice field

Behind Grandma's home we played,

Skipped stones, picked flowers,

Their petals uglier than their thorns.

My friends beckoned me to join,

But I heard my stomach grumble

You shan't join, it said.

You don't belong there, it whispered.

I was right—

They did leave me without further ado.

From there I began to wonder,

If my only solace was a mango tree,

I swore I'd ne'er miss it to infinity.

I was wrong—

Something crashed,

It pulled me to the moment

When the winner took it all.

I wasn't there—

To join in their soaring win,

To be that kid once again,

To not know what lies ahead,

And what will become of me.

Chapter II
Flora and Fauna

Venus Flytrap

O'er your slimy leaf I crawled

sweet nectar, so inviting,

your luscious teeth were waiting,

snap trap, what a booby trap!

Sharp bristles caught me

in one embrace;

I was swallowed, unfazed,

in one sharpless toothy gulp!

The countdown began like any other—

one pause,

two side to sides,

three kisses,

now I want to hide!

Twigs o' Fiddle

O'er the branches of a narra tree

where flowers bloom so free.

An 'ol dear kingfisher sits atop,

alone and dreary.

What're you looking for? I wonder.

minnows 'n sticklebacks?

Oh, 'ol dear kingfisher,

wait for your turn.

Keep your song for a little while,

ne'er hurry, blessed are those who tarry.

Rustic

Lo! Look at thy eyes, wanderer!

Cows grazing, tamaraws bowing,

Under the sun's heat, no farmer can't beat.

Would you prefer the noise of a bustling metro?

Would you rejoice at the smell of daisies in the meadow?

'Tis nature's way of paradox

In each equinox, the countryside stays the same

I'd choose a sun's ray o'er any other.

Verdant

I had a dream so teal—

little girls in their tutus walked past,

their hair pale against the midday sun.

I had a dream so green—

thick as the foliage surrounding a pavilion

next to the boardwalk where crowds gather.

I had a dream so lime—

around a verdant semi-circle,

people dance, sing, and laugh.

Glory Cedar

Madre de cacao

mahamot mo na bulak

maberdeng dahon

nami sa akon mata

katahum 'di malimtan.

*

[English Translation]

Glory cedar

Your fragrant petals

Sage green leaves

Beautiful in my eyes

A pulchritude I will never forget.

Que sera, sera

Quiet is loud, can you see—

how owls stalk their prey?

why spiders weave every day?

Que sera, sera, this life is ours—

why settle for one era

if you can live for all hours?

Que sera, sera, one span of a decade,

'tis short if well-played,

only in tranquility, a self can be found.

Chapter III

Encounters

A Fisherman's Lament

One week's worth fishing

left me in utter despair

limbs aching, back burnt;

in the horizon, I heard

a beckoning siren song.

I sat, craned my neck

on a stilted sea shanty

intrigued 'n yearning

to hear that sweet gypsy voice

dance, tiptoe above the waves.

Aboard a dinghy,

I sailed across a stormy sea

enchanted to see

the gypsy's unbothered lair

amidst a raging cold breeze.

Troubled gusts o' winds

deep in the ocean, I found

a lonely cavern

o' my beautiful gypsy

lady, where shall I find thee?

Graceful melody

startling, awake on its own

I found thee floating

hands in bosoms, eyelids closed

did I really hear ye sing?

Love of Yore

I

How do I taste thee?

beet red lips, sweet as berries

puckered in response

when I spoke epiphanies

how do I declare such love?

II

Quit the tease thine love

lo! don't follow me yonder

where eyes lurk behind

sequoias bathed in moonshine

come, let us tarry instead.

Lush

Velvet touch, rainy kisses trail down your arched neck,

down to the hidden crevices of your bosoms.

Shiver without abandon, uninhibited,

you grip me twice, once in the hair, twice in the biceps.

Whispers of assent, lips dance more than meet,

immeasurable against every move of our hips, waists, hands!

Oh, how they traverse the valleys of navel and mounds,

we shan't wait for dawn to come.

We shall tarry, hurry, hurry, hurry,

clocks tick our final precipice to heavens!

Tremors

I have kept these emotions at bay

(I could bear it no more)

I'd rather hide from your pretty face

(I'd rather speak of it herefore)

Lub-dubs make me dizzy

(Lub-dubs turn my brain into frenzy)

Girl, I want to cave in

(I don't wish for you to go mean)

Bottled-up, like whiskey in a barrel

(Uninhibited, like a waterfall unravel)

Tremors spread over my chest

(Lest I look in my best)

Hard-boiled Heartbeats

Call it dreaming, we linger along the edges

Of surreal. Lost in repentance

Against anything we've done wrong.

Polar opposites rarely do

Make a good match. Two ends clash,

We both know how it ends–

Our laughter lost its luster, jokes turned

Sour. They left a bitter taste

On our mouths. Your hands reached for

Mine. 'Twas too late!

Open-ended tête-à-têtes forsook their tune.

Now we speak

In distant, lukewarm stares. Our paths began

To cleave as lightning would strike

The sky in white gray tendrils. Lovely paramour,

'Tis a love of rainbows to

Turmoil, turbulence, turgid tenacity.

'Tis no surprise we dig to

Look for rabbit holes. Will you be

Alright, darling? Will you

Succumb to your stolid state? Until when–

I dare ask–will our

Heartbeats cease? Will their rhythmic

Lub-Dubs turn to flatlines?

We See Red

Banish from my thoughts!

oh dear, what did I do?

oh darling, what did you do?

Like baneberries,

hate spat fire to our love

dust to must, we crumbled.

Shook me from my dream!

lest it turned to nightmares,

lest demons breathe once more.

Farewell thee, sprinkles!

I bid thou bitter byes.

Providence

Piercing gaze, so enticing,

Come closer so I can see what you're hiding.

Do you not know?

Your late Wednesday nights hide your teen lovers in a burrow.

Darling, this rabbit hole unfurls in a sudden revelation,

Don't make me find your other girls.

Treacherous Hearts

Try as I might,

your betrayal sliced through

with nothing but fright.

What can I do?

this wound brought pain,

so skin-deep, lacerations not few.

Undid, fastened to your love

like a kite, I'm a fool

to a promise for two.

Hoodwinked

Come hither, sly cunning fox

Your mask slips when no one's looking

Words of affirmation, so orthodox,

Everyone draws near when you're howling.

You met me when my sorrow was deepest,

Tamed me like other foxes,

I followed without protest

Until the day I realized your hoaxes.

Come on, you love me when I beg

Come on, you love to judge the weak,

Unencumbered, naïve, tiny foxes.

Who can understand but you?

Who else but you can comfort us?

Give me one more wink, crinkle, tickle,

Sloe-eyed, so sweet, such deceit,

A demon spawn, a fallen angel,

Tell me, sly cunning fox,

Are you what you really are?

Outlier

Dainty lovely Missy

Unapologetic, false beauty,

A true-blooded know-it-all.

Willy peers in the dark, watching,

His mouth curls in disdain.

He rolls his eyes, scoffing—

She'll never be a wife to any man;

A lady shan't speak when hushed,

A lady shan't dress in a man's clothes.

Missy shall sing to him

In soft, sweet lullabies

To be the apple of his eyes.

Dissenter, outlier,

Eccentric, electric,

No decent man will ever come.

What's there to see?

Missy's pert bosoms,

Skewed nose, ugly bottoms.

Willy furrows his brow;

Unladylike, so brash, such insolence!

Willy shakes his head without repent.

Drunk in prejudice, Willy perished

With his own noose wrapped around

His neck, thighs, hands unbound.

The curse dies with the tormentor,

Whilst Missy sails very deep, beyond the seas.

There! She'll be a woman of nobodies.

The Big Bad Wolf

I know you

You enslave women

With sugared words

Dipped in pixies of persuasion.

I know you

You're the man behind the mask

The animal hiding beneath the skin

Of a shy charming sheep.

I know you

You are blessed with wits

To conquer the innocent.

I know you

You whisper decadent songs

To lure women under your feet

You are the Big Bad Wolf

You can take any shape

Any animal you want to morph into.

These girls you made your victims

They are not your playthings

They are humans

Blood, flesh, and bones

Built for the same purpose as you.

If you ever meet the Big Bad Wolf

Do not run

Do not fight

Listen to your gut

What does it say?

Fight or flight

The choice is yours.

Upside Down

A gamut of fear began to sprout

My darling, how could you?

Whilst you were away with your lover,

I sat among cypress trees and cower.

You turned me upside down,

With manicured nails, twisted frowns.

I handed sarcasm on a clean platter,

But you mistook it a blabber.

A wretched loss in my palate,

Dear mademoiselle, lest you forget.

Moth to a Flame

Why did you blame the moth

For being too arrogant,

Conceited to fly around the flame.

If you see it the other way

The moth mustn't be tamed

One attracts the wrong crowd

Jumping to conclusions

As Icarus would do the same

Sometimes words can only

Shadow what's behind the veil

Who are you hiding from?

What did you mean by that?

Questions linger around you

In incandescent murmurs.

When the moth's wings flutter close,

Take a step back,

Reinvent and peer closely,

Is it the moth or the flame?

Where does the fault lie?

Would you look again?

Whisper to me

Who needs a pregnant pause?

The moth or the flame?

Once Upon a Pipe Dream

Give or take,

that's what happens when you love,

or is it?

To like from afar,

to feel the tingle of nerves

traveling down your spine.

What did you see?

a happy mirage or tragedy?

Infatuation is only a trick,

a ruse of the brain's weird pathways.

This wishful thinking

will get you nowhere;

for who are you to like—

someone you can't reach?

someone you can't touch nor see?

someone your mind can only paint?

Chapter IV

The Citizen

Zarathustra's Mark

Spirit of fire, heart like a stone,

Such is a man named Zarathustra.

Old in the soul, always alone,

Searching for wisdom in plethora.

He climbs down the mountains,

Bids valediction to his solitude.

Deep in the lowlands, lashing rains,

Unfettered with the steep altitude.

Zarathustra arrives in town,

Heart full, mind agog,

Only to see the meltdowns,

Frowns, murmurs, and hiss.

The people demand his judgments,

Ubermensch! Ubermensch!

Each with growing temperaments,

Are they chaos or dancing stars?

Zarathustra mounts his steed,

Indeed, a fellow knight will say,

Oh, lad! Tell us what you did.

There on the mountains, away from fray.

He speaks for the crowd,

Naysayers clamor for noises,

They mock, cluck, rock

Their heels and voices.

Silence plummets, hush descends,

Omnipresent Overman, Supreme Superman,

Live dangerously, he says, *plant the seed of your highest hope,*

Behold! Don't fret for I shall show you the Last Man.

A Shade for the Future

Do you not care?

One circle is a vote for the people of this nation

Do you only mind your own lair?

If the crocs are waiting for victory,

Why can't we sew our knitted hearts?

Wear our protest proudly on our sleeves?

Would you remain idle?

Waiting for the next voting to begin?

Would you remain stoic amidst this storm?

Do you think of farmers toiling their lands with promises of small returns?

Do you think of children sleeping behind rotten fruit boxes?

Do you think of women being harassed in a dark alley?

Why? Can't you see the change this country wants?

Why? Do you have to keep your eyes shut to the crocs' turpitude?

Why? Do you remain silent?

Chapter V
Odes

Absolute than Kismet

Two babes sprung from two different wombs,

The fathers swore, the mothers laughed,

An age-old miracle set in stone.

These two little angels will dance

When the clock strikes at its decisive moment.

What will Cupid say?

Predestined or not, when the time comes,

When stars and planets coalesce into one,

Their light will be brighter than the sun.

Yin and Yang

Past, present, future

All blur into a void.

When I see you in déjà vus,

I'm reminded of hidden touches,

Moonlit kisses,

Dainty wishes.

If I could bring forth

These memories of you today,

I would build a monument

To honor our love

Till the very last sprigs of May.

It is but a bumpy road ahead,

Full of patches,

Littered with wounds left untreated.

Will you take the chance again?

Will I accept you till the very end?

Memento for a Special Girl

You weren't there when I first saw you.

Your wise years will guide you,

From this small Pacific island

To the cornfields of Iowa,

Our hearts will follow.

Deep in my heart,

I know this bond will never break.

It's not unfair to go away,

Life may demand more from us,

But we will still be the same.

The same college girls—

Who go crazy over K-dramas,

Fictional men,

Smut books,

That's us.

I am happy and thankful

For meeting a friend like you

Geography will not dare take us apart,

No matter how far or long,

You will always be my bosom friend.

You are one of the queens I shall not forget,

Life can be cruel sometimes,

But this gift of friendship I will treasure—

Till the end of time

Till we see the women we have become.

Queens of Themyscira

Some say Wonder Woman belongs to the pretty popular,

I choose to differ—they are everywhere—

Thick thighs, lush mouths,

Straight and curly hair,

With bodies wired for battle.

Some with feline eyes that speak of the fire within

Others with ember voices that can spark fire when they sing

Hear their lullabies, their lost hopes and far-fetched dreams

When I see them from my past,

I will nod my head, even bow to them.

These queens of Themyscira I adore

For being brave, smart, and keen.

I will tell you this at once—

If you see a Wonder Woman,

Will you listen to her pounding chest?

Will you turn your head and walk away?

A Wonder Woman knows who she is

Her skin, bones, and blood make up her wings

Her beliefs and truths pump air to her lungs

She is fierce but careless, radical but good-natured.

If she is a paradox,

Then who are you to say you know her?

Abysmal

The mind dictates whilst the heart follows

You cannot betray me with your absence

My soaked cheeks prod your grey eyes to open,

Lifeless, numb, your limbs unmoving.

I cannot bear to lose the rhythmic thump of a lively soul

I clutch your hand, clammy and cold,

I shiver and draw you in

Spice, smoke—that's what you are to me.

You have left this world as quick as a flash of lightning,

For years I have cried over what ifs and could have beens

You were a bitter pill to swallow or—

A beacon for me to follow to another life.

Kaleidoscope

Visions of red and blue, I see you

In bits of mirrorlike images

Raven-haired, chocolate skin

I'd love to see it shine in the evening sun.

Each year I could wish

A thousand patterns of you in my mind

But what's left coalesce to shapes.

You're a bit of a parallelogram

Bent upon days of happiness

Failures and setbacks.

You're a pentagram

With your pointy stubborn streaks.

You're an oval

Forever catching thoughts

In a cycle of 365 days.

Your dreams have gathered

In a jar of shapes

Collected inside mirrors reflecting each other.

I'd love to see your lines, your angles.

In a kaleidoscope, I glimpse the real you.

A Writer's Oasis

The cadence of words is sweet,

Honeyed and weaved through endless spins of time.

I can't remember when

But words speak to me

As if I can hear them soft and loud.

Some clash and break,

Others flow like a river,

Luminous and strung tight.

I can hear them,

The voices of unsung stories.

They need to be told,

But is anyone around?

Epilogue

Nights in Sonder City is a different type of experimentation. Poetry is unfamiliar to me. I tried to steer away from it because of some limitations. A poem needs rhymes, meter, caesura; but every once in a while, a muse will toss more ideas into the pile. It came one early morning in between projects when words were scarce, short . . . sort of fleeting. It's a strange expression of thought compared to writing prose. When everything is at rest, you can hear the words forming–how they shape a verse into something profound and beautiful.

Each verse reflects a state of mind. *Nights in Sonder City* can mean anything to anyone. To some, it's good and exhilarating; to others, it's predictable and boring. These tales are both real and illusory. As Stephen King once said, "The muses are ghosts, and sometimes they come uninvited."

Don't miss out!

Visit the website below and you can sign up to receive emails whenever Liezl Villanueva publishes a new book. There's no charge and no obligation.

https://books2read.com/r/B-A-XZZDB-XPHDD

BOOKS 2 READ

Connecting independent readers to independent writers.

Did you love *Nights in Sonder City*? Then you should read *Cosmic Threads* by Liezl Villanueva!

The Big Bang happened around 13.7 billion years ago. One cataclysmic event drew the future of planets, galaxies, asteroids, Earth, and humans. These tiny specks in the universe formed cosmic threads. Love, anger, sorrow, lust began to bloom, fade, and blossom again. Is humanity ready yet, or will they look up for a moment?

Read more at https://thehatcheries.wordpress.com.

About the Author

Liezl Villanueva is a writer based in the Philippines. When she is not writing, you can find her in the countryside, dreaming of other worlds with her mountain bike. Her work has previously appeared in Open Door Poetry Magazine.

Read more at https://thehatcheries.wordpress.com.

Milton Keynes UK
Ingram Content Group UK Ltd.
UKHW020126070524
442290UK00014BC/577